The Embellisher: Let's Get Started!

Myfanwy Hart

Techniques for needle felting using
The Embellisher machine, suitable
sewing machine attachments,
hand-felting equipment, and
introducing Nuvo Felt

Design & Photography By Preface Studios Ltd
www.prefacestudios.com
info@prefacestudios.com

Published in 2006 by
M & J Enterprises
17 Elms Road
Fleet
Hampshire
GU51 3EG
UK

Telephone: 01252 617667
sales@sassalynne.com
www.sassalynne.com

Printed in Great Britain by
Borcombe SP
Premier Way
Abbey Park Industrial Estate
Romsey
Hampshire
SO51 9AQ

A CIP record is registered by and held at the British Library

ISBN: 0-9553932-0-5

Dedication

This book is dedicated to my long-suffering husband, who has kept me on the straight and narrow, especially when everything seemed to go wrong and I just about gave up! It is also dedicated to my mother who has supported me in everything that I have ever tried to do.

Acknowledgments:

With grateful thanks to Sally Brockbank whose stitching skills par excellence saved the day.

With admiration and thanks to Helen Hadley who managed so much in so short a time whilst still suffering from jet lag.

CONTENTS

Introduction 2 - 3

1: Materials 4 - 6

2: Let's Get Started 7 - 11

3: Texture for Fabrics 12 - 15

4: Entrapment 16 - 17

5: Working With Wool 18 - 21

6: Knitting Is Back 22 - 26

7: Adding Your Own Colour 27 - 31

8: Fabulous Fibres 32 - 34

9: Nuvo Felt 35 - 40

10: What Now? 41 - 42

Suppliers 43

What does it mean 'to embellish'?

The Oxford English Dictionary says:

> to embellish means beautify, adorn

Merrian-Webster's Collegiate Dictionary gives it two meanings:

> to make beautiful with ornamentation
> to heighten the attractiveness of by adding ornamental details

Chambers Dictionary defines it as:

> a way to beautify something with decoration

This is what we are exploring.

Introduction

So, what is an Embellisher?

At first glance it looks like a small sewing machine. It is about the same shape, size and weight, however taking a closer look, you will see that instead of one needle there are more (my machine has seven). None of these needles has an eye, which means NO THREADING! There is also a foot pedal, and depressing it will cause the needles to rise and fall in just the same way as a sewing machine.

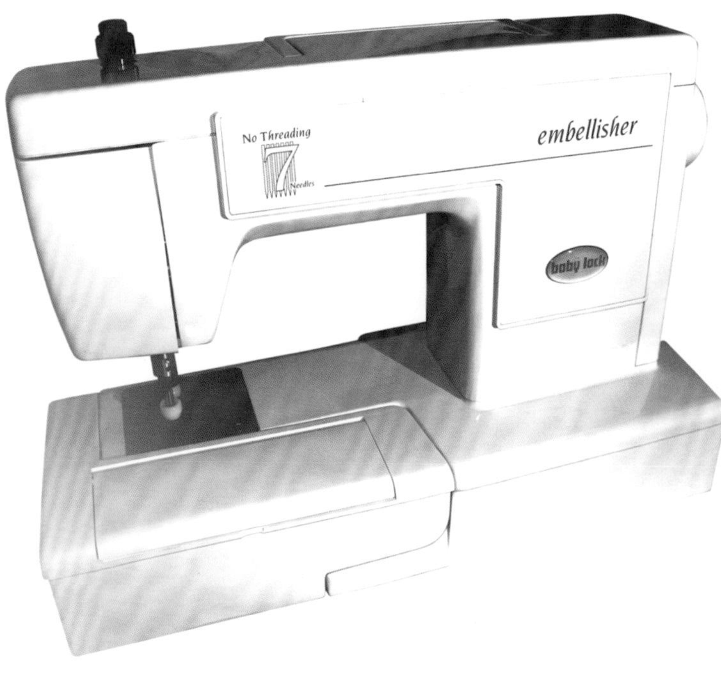

The needles, though, have barbs, if you *gently* touch them you will feel them but DO NOT DO THIS WHILE THE MACHINE IS CONNECTED TO THE POWER SOURCE OR IS IN MOTION. These barbs are actually the 'business' parts. As the needles pass through the fibres, fabric etc, the barbs agitate and mesh them together. Just a few seconds sitting in front of the machine will show how quick and easy it is. You will soon be 'hooked'!

I have to be honest! I wanted an Embellisher before I had even seen one! I first saw an advert for one in an American publication, but couldn't find any information in the UK. Imagine my delight, then, when I saw one at a show in Exeter. It was expensive, and I had to use all my wiles to persuade my husband to allow me to indulge. Fortunately the exhibitor was equally persuasive and between us we succeeded! It could so easily have been a white elephant, but instead it opened a door to a whole new experience and another means of using many of the skills that I had previously learnt.

So many owners of an Embellisher have told me that they have purchased the machine but don't know what to do with it. Some even said that they were scared to take off the cover. Consequently, I was inspired to write this book and I hope that it will encourage you not only to have a go at the featured techniques but also to experiment with new ways to use this fascinating machine.

CHAPTER: 1

Materials

Materials

The materials used are many and varied. Some of them will be introduced in the following pages, but this list is just to whet your appetite!

Yarns:

Thick, thin, silk, cotton, rayon, nylon, polyester, metallised polyester, raffia, novelty yarns etc.

Fibres:

Wool, silk, cotton, viscose, bamboo, soy, mohair, alpaca, cashmere, sisal, blends of any of these, to name just a few! Silk Carrier Rod Waste can also be used, especially if broken down into layers.

Novelty fibres:

Angelina fibre (also sometimes called Angel Hair), both the Standard and Hot Fix colours work well. Trilobal Nylon can also be added to other fibres etc for interesting effects.

Fabrics:

Wool, silk, cotton, felt, polyester, nylon etc. Dupion silk or butter muslin and scrim are just as useful, they can be used in their own right or as backgrounds for further embellishing.

Temporary Sprays

These sprays are designed to hold items in place while working but disappear after a while, consequently not altering the handle of fabric. The spray that I use is called 505 and is available worldwide. It is not needed for all techniques, but worth bearing in mind.

Soluble Fabrics

All soluble fabrics may be of use at some point but the one that I have found to be invaluable is SoluWeb. Very much lighter than the others it dissolves immediately with just a light spray. It is not suitable for some sewing techniques, but is Ideal for use as described in the following pages.

This is just a small selection of the materials that I have tried. I am sure you will find more, but if you have even a few of these you *can* get started!

Extra Equipment

A soldering iron or heat tool could be useful for further manipulating your work. Hand felting needles (preferably in a holder or with a handle) and a piece of foam, are useful for manipulating 3D shapes, and can also be used for most of the techniques mentioned in this book if the embellisher is not to hand. Further decoration can be added using either machine or hand stitching.

The felting needles are fairly robust, and breakages can be avoided by being careful. Steer clear of yarns and threads etc that have elements of metal, (some threads are only metallised polyester, they are fine) and also those that are too hard or thick.

No Embellisher? Do it by hand!

Dry needle-felting has been around for some time, and is in fact an adaptation of an industrial technique. Similar effects to those described in this book can also be created by hand using a holder with one or more needles. A foam pad is also required, and for safety work within a container, for example a small box or seed tray. Working this way will take longer but is still enjoyable.

CHAPTER: 2

Let's Get Started

Let's Get Started

The machine that I have is made by BabyLock. There are other machines; however I have been unable to view these for a variety of reasons. There are also attachments for various sewing machines, but it is possible that some of them have been discontinued. This book is not written to publicise a particular make, or to imply that one machine is better than another, it is purely to introduce a few techniques. My machine is very robust; I have used it for several hours at a time and it has withstood the use of many different surfaces.

The beauty of an embellisher is that it is just so easy to create an effect. It will transform anything that is placed under the needles, and this means that, at least to begin with, it isn't necessary to purchase specific materials! You will probably have everything you need for your first trials. These first few steps will give you a collection of samples to which you can refer time and time again. I tend to use my machine to make backgrounds for further embellishment, however, pieces could be so stunning that they don't need any further work.

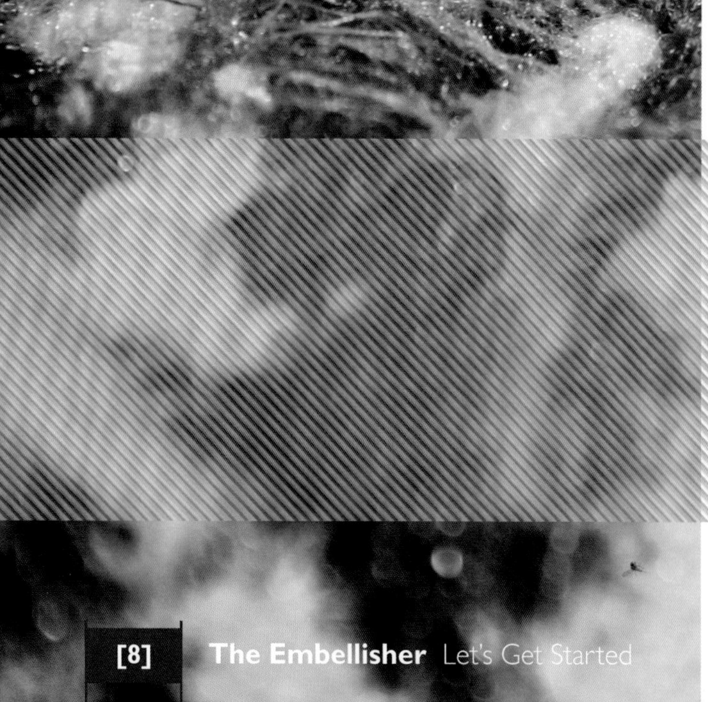

My first experiments involved purchased felt. It is cheap and, frankly, often just lying around waiting to be used. Felt is a good stable surface for the embellisher, and can be used without an embroidery hoop, making it ideal for quick experiments. Yarns of most thicknesses are suitable, and this is a good opportunity to use some that were acquired for a long-forgotten idea or intention. Have a look in shops and at shows, there are many suitable knitting yarns currently on sale, the picture below shows just a small selection.

Don't pull or move too fast, the needles will break if too much force is used, and you don't want to have to change one already!

The process of working with the needles is called 'meshing'. As you mesh the fibres together more and more they will also be pushed to the underside of the felt. It is worth looking at this, maybe the effects produced on the underside are more suited to your needs than the top. Very subtle effects can be produced this way.

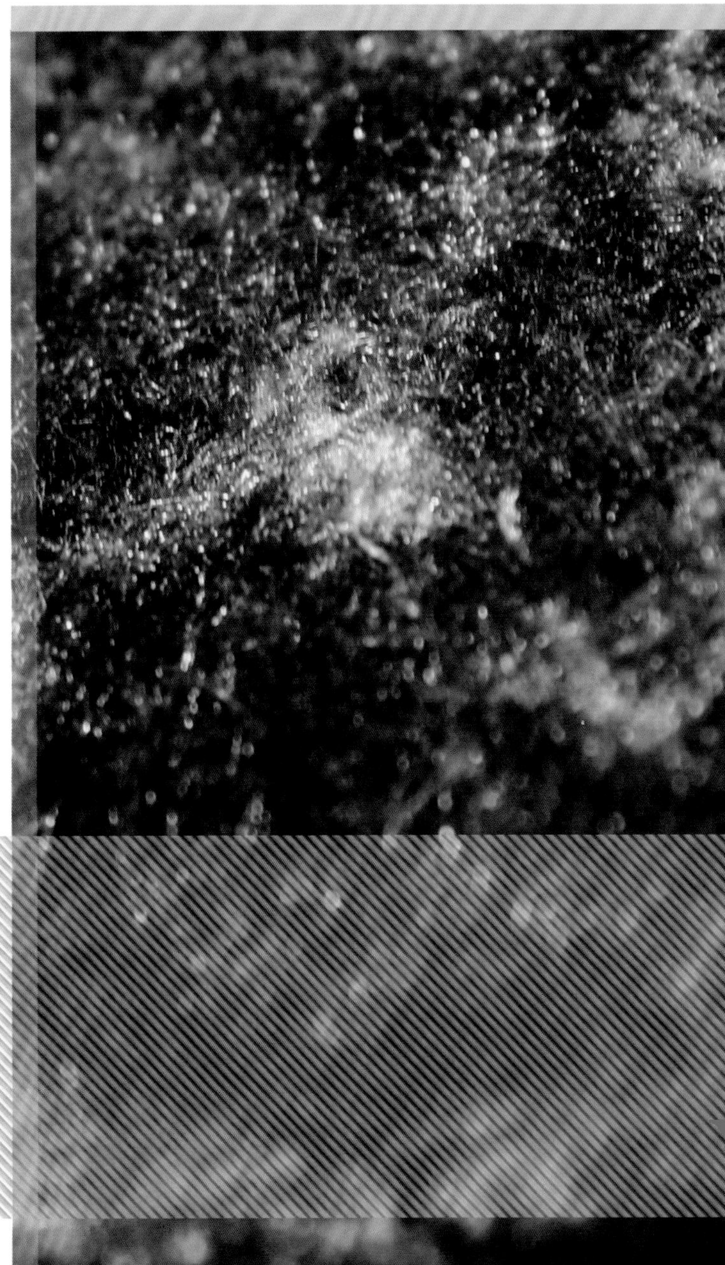

Don't consider only the chunky yarns; some of the finer ones are equally useful. You will be surprised at just what can be used; the fine ones with flags of nylon paper are as useful as loosely twisted woollen roving. Feel free to experiment.

Take a piece of felt:

- Cut various yarns, fabrics etc into small pieces.
- Scatter them on top and place under the needles.
- Lower the needles and depress the foot pedal.
- Gently guide the felt in various directions under the needles.

If your work becomes jammed, don't worry or panic. Stop. Lift the lever to raise the needles, and then gently stretch your work by holding at each side edge. This is usually all that is needed, occasionally, however, just a little more' pulling power' is required.

The fabric you are creating can be moved in all directions as you work. Doing this really 'massages' the fibres/yarns into the under layer. You will see, later in the chapter, that it is possible to manipulate your work thereby creating more texture. Use these initial experiments to practice the movements. If you have learnt to operate a sewing machine for creative free embroidery you will not have trouble, the actions are very similar. If this concept is new to you it will soon become 'second nature'.

The beauty of the BabyLock Embellisher is that you can run the machine off the edge of the fabric, which means that you can work up to and well into the edge. This technique is worth practicing. At first I was frustrated that the needles did not stop in the 'up' position. Now I just run the machine up and over the edge. Doing this stops a ridge from forming which could be unsightly.

Try the same exercise mentioned previously but this time use butter muslin or scrim instead of felt. If you have enough, use the same selection of yarns as before, the results will be different and comparisons useful.

Undulating surfaces can be made by meshing in circles. Working round and round from the centre to the outside will produce 'hills'; starting at the outside of the circle and working towards the centre will make a valley. This can be quite fun and is a technique worth practicing.

It is worth looking for unusual yarns. The sample below shows a yarn with a feathery fringe on both sides. It has only been meshed down the centre to make the most of the fringe. A flat tape like yarn will give a completely different effect, so too would a ribbon yarn.

SKETCHBOOK

Collect all your samples as you play then file them in a ring folder or sketchbook with, perhaps, a note or two. Suitably filed they will become a useful reference source.

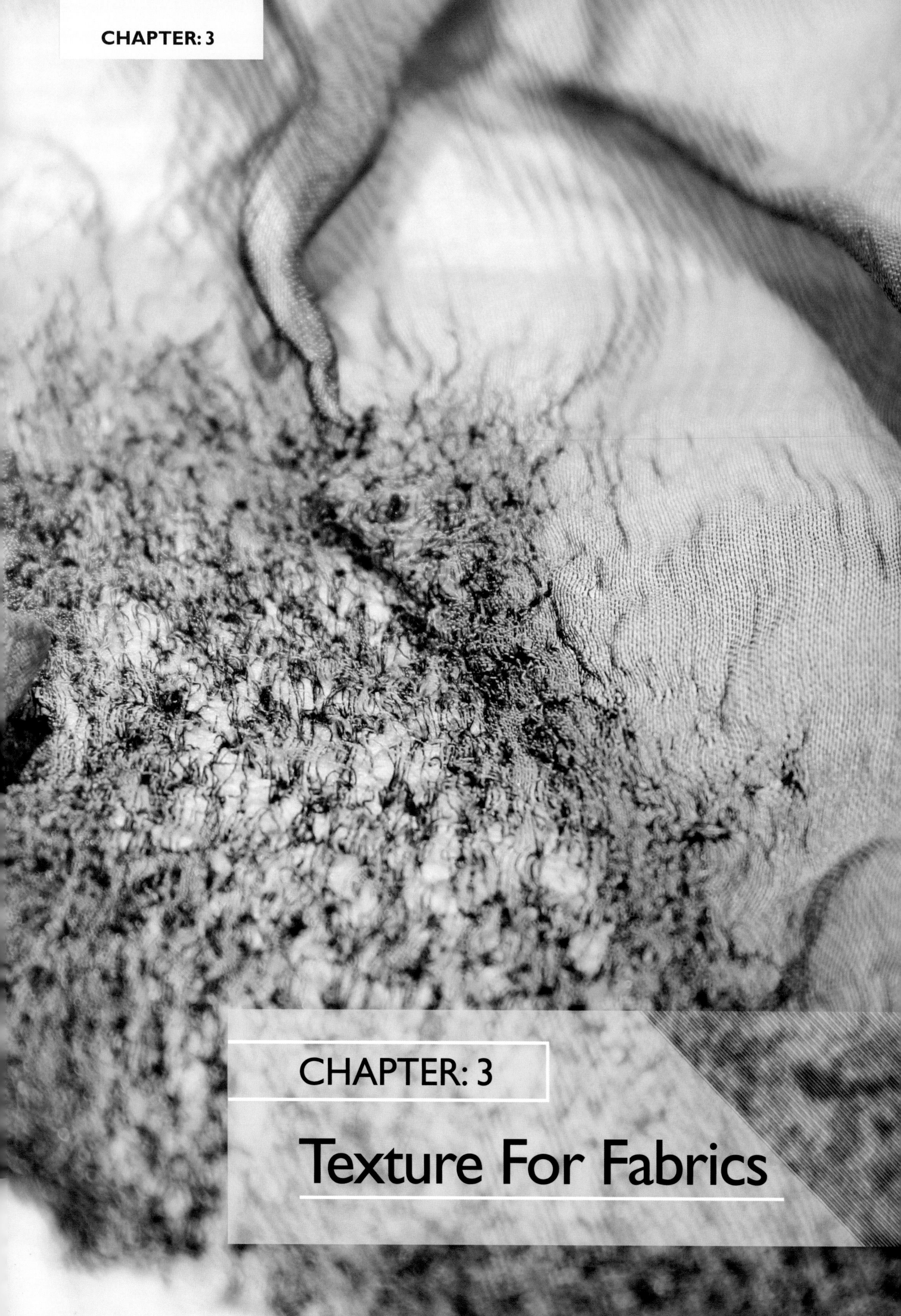

CHAPTER: 3

Texture For Fabrics

Texture For Fabrics

If you haven't thought of using the embellisher to create texture try it now and you will be delighted. Just working on something as mundane as a piece of nylon organza will show how easy it is to alter the surface of a fabric. There are many to try, and don't forget to include the manmade and silk metallic tissues that are available.

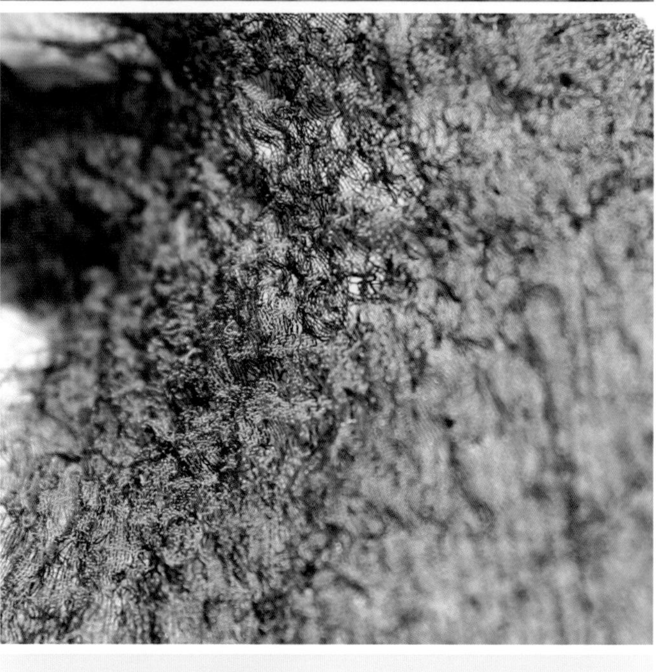

Experiment by meshing as many types of fabric as possible at first. This will produce a stash of manipulated fabrics which can later either be cut and added to further work, or used as a background surface in its own right.

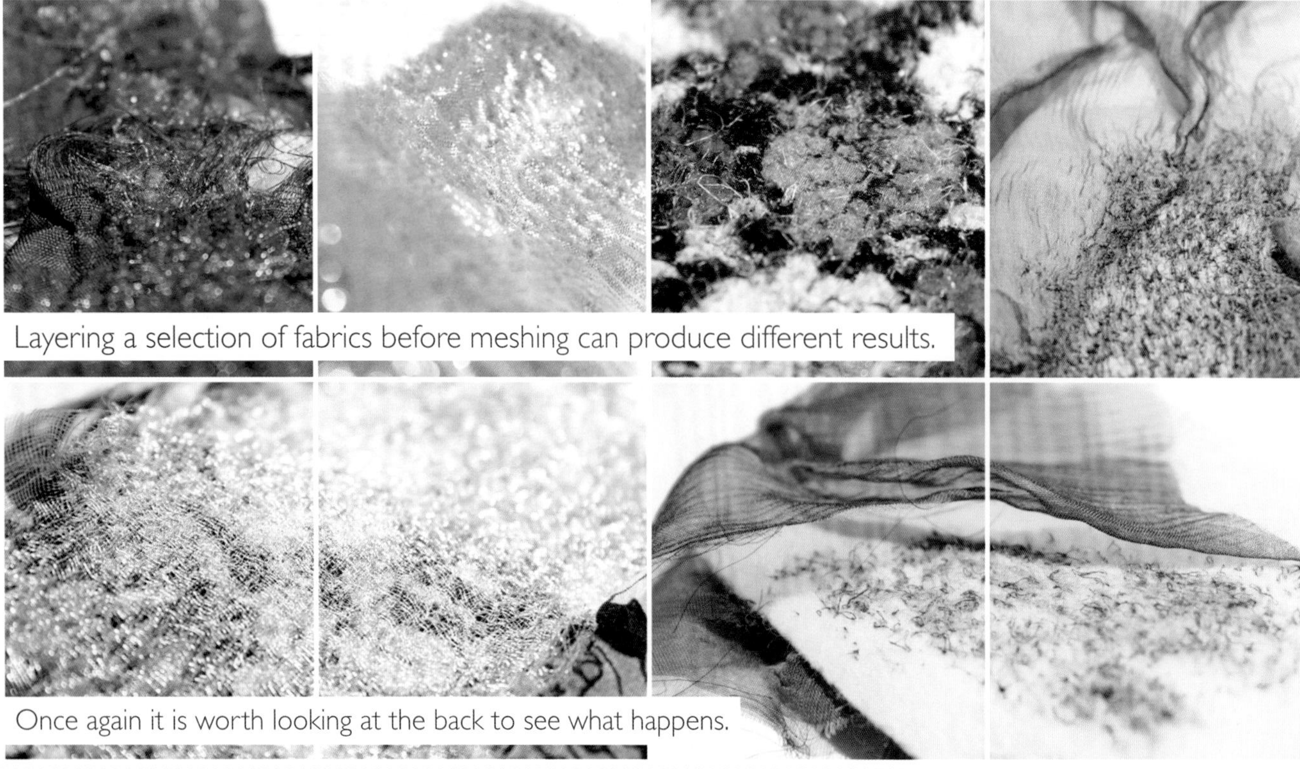

Layering a selection of fabrics before meshing can produce different results.

Once again it is worth looking at the back to see what happens.

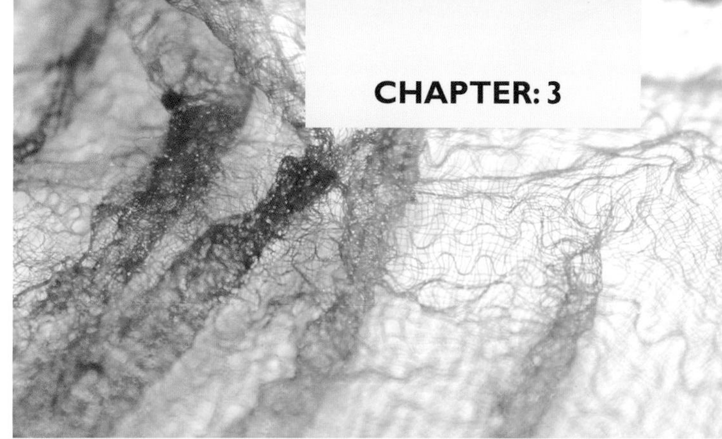

Pleating is another way to create texture. Normally pleats would be stitched using the sewing machine but folding fabric and then manipulating it along the fold with the embellisher produces an interesting crumpled effect. This is especially effective on lightweight fabrics, including the ubiquitous chiffon scarf; the latter can be overlaid in its pleated state creating even more texture. Pleating on both the top and underside of fabric will also alter the appearance.

For another lovely effect:

Choose several chiffon scarves in co-ordinating colours (there are three in the sample below). Each should be a square about 30 cm x 30 cm (12 ins x 12 ins). You will also need a piece of base fabric of your choice about twice the size of a postcard.

1. Cut each square of chiffon into strips approx 3cm (1½ ins) wide.
2. Fold a strip in half along its length and mesh along the folded edge only
3. Fray the loose edges using a pin.
4. Repeat the last two steps with all the other strips of chiffon.
5. The chiffon strips are now ready to be meshed to the base fabric. They will be layered so that the frayed edge disguises the meshed edge of its neighbour.
6. Start on the left-hand side of the base fabric. Position a strip of chiffon with the fraying overhanging the edge. Mesh from top to bottom along the previously folded edge.
7. Place the second strip to the right of the first, the frayed edge should cover the last meshed edge. Secure the folded edge with the embellisher again working from top to bottom.
8. Fill the base fabric in this way, varying the colour of chiffon.

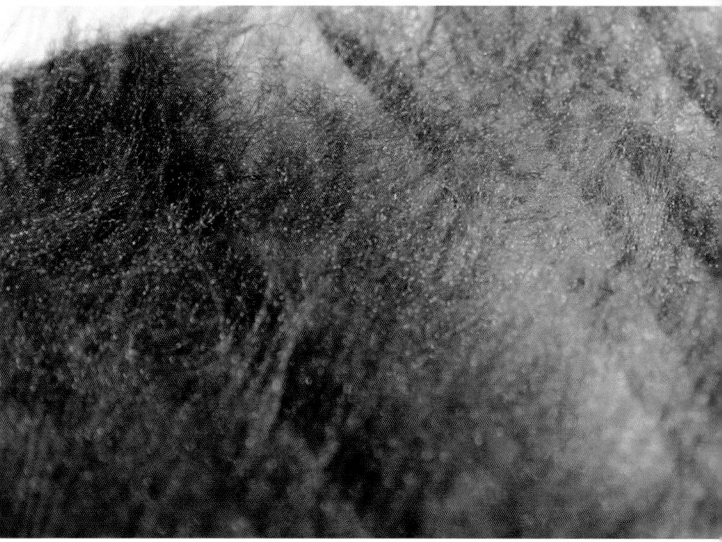

Further effects can be obtained by scattering small cut pieces of chiffon over the base fabric before attaching the 'fringes'. Secure them lightly so they don't move around too much.

The strips can also be applied without fraying. Place the strips close together for a very frilly surface.

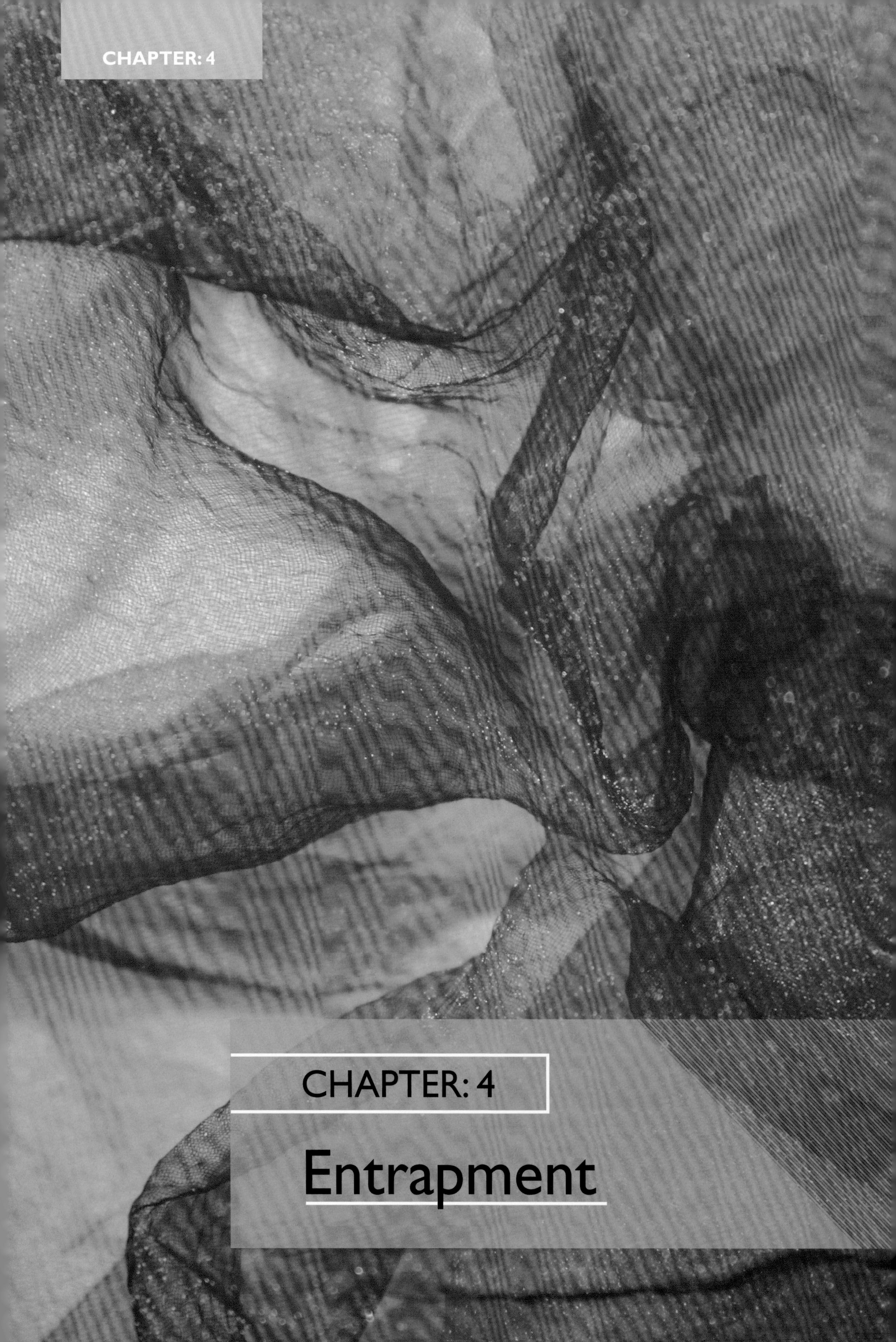

CHAPTER: 4

Entrapment

Entrapment

We have seen that nylon chiffon scarves are a useful addition to the workbox. Extremely light and almost completely transparent they are available in a range of colours and can be used in a variety of textile techniques. They are equally invaluable when used with the Embellisher.

There are a number of ways in which I like to use chiffon scarves, and we will meet them again later. If the right colour is chosen they can become almost invisible. This makes them ideal for covering and anchoring items that cannot be meshed. Items such as small pieces of metal shim, feathers, and skeleton leaves can be held in place while the area around is dealt with. Don't forget, too, that areas can be cut from the chiffon using a soldering iron to reveal areas, or your work could be manipulated with a heat gun.

Partly exposed metal, shell, etc, would make an interesting contrast in both colour and texture. Sandwiching skeleton leaves between 2 layers of chiffon could make an attractive wall hanging or curtain for a small window, for example. The area between the leaves could be meshed, and possibly decorated further with hand or machine stitching.

Small pieces of handmade or other paper could also be held in place in this way, so too beautiful pieces of lace. Cheap lace is an interesting cover for fibres or yarns, when meshed these show through the lace making an unusual surface texture.

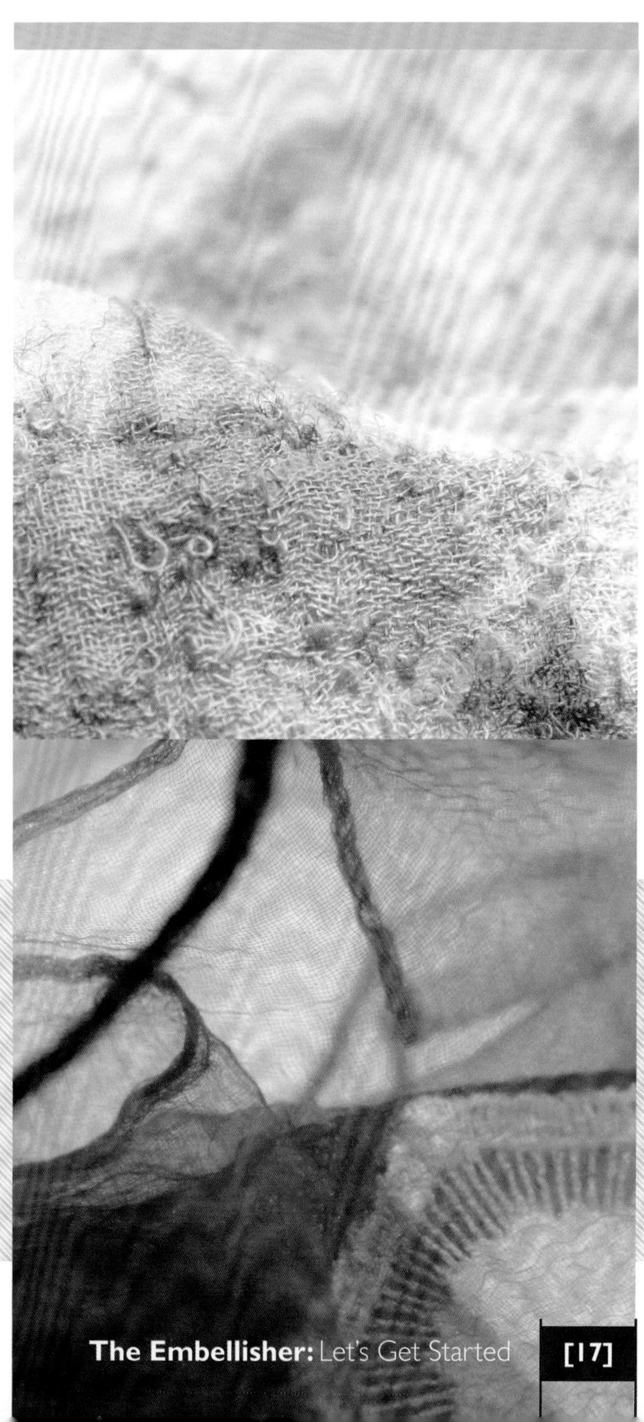

CHAPTER: 5

Working with Wool

Working With Wool

Wool is available in a number of forms. Woollen fabrics make excellent backgrounds. The surface texture of woven wool can be transformed under the needles of the embellisher. It can produce a really densely felted fabric, or a lightweight, almost flimsy, material.

Threads can be withdrawn from areas of loosely woven wool before meshing. These threads can be rewoven elsewhere to create denser areas, or placed on top of the same or another piece as an added embellishment.

Yarns and fibres can be built up into wonderful surfaces, purely by scattering them on areas and meshing them together. These pieces can then be used in their own right as backgrounds or cut up and rearranged to make more complex surfaces. As always two surfaces are produced at once. The under surface is usually more subtle than the top and choosing the one to use can sometimes be a problem!

One of my favourite techniques is to use lightly spun woollen yarn. The first one that I tried was Point 5 by Colinette. This is an uneven yarn, thick and thin, which is hand-dyed. Some of the colours are beautifully subtle, some rich and vibrant, but all delightful in their own right. The thicker slubs can be pulled apart to create random areas of texture. I began by placing two strands next to each other and just worked down the length, meshing along the join. It was quite quick to build up a piece of multicoloured felt.

Another of my favourite yarns is Caldo from Lana Grossa. More like a thin woollen roving than a traditional knitting yarn it can be pulled apart very easily. Breaking the lengths down is equally easy and ideal when filling in small areas. The picture below shows a small sample made with Caldo.

Yarns were just laid on a background fabric in a swirly pattern and the spaces between filled in with other yarn.

Using this method make several small pieces of felt in a variety of co-ordinating colours.

1. Choose one that is a little larger for the background.
2. Cut shapes from the others.
3. Arrange the pieces and mesh again to integrate them.

Another suggestion is to make two pieces of felt, again in co-ordinating colours.

1. Make cuts and slashes in one
2. Place it on top of the other. Mesh the two surfaces together.

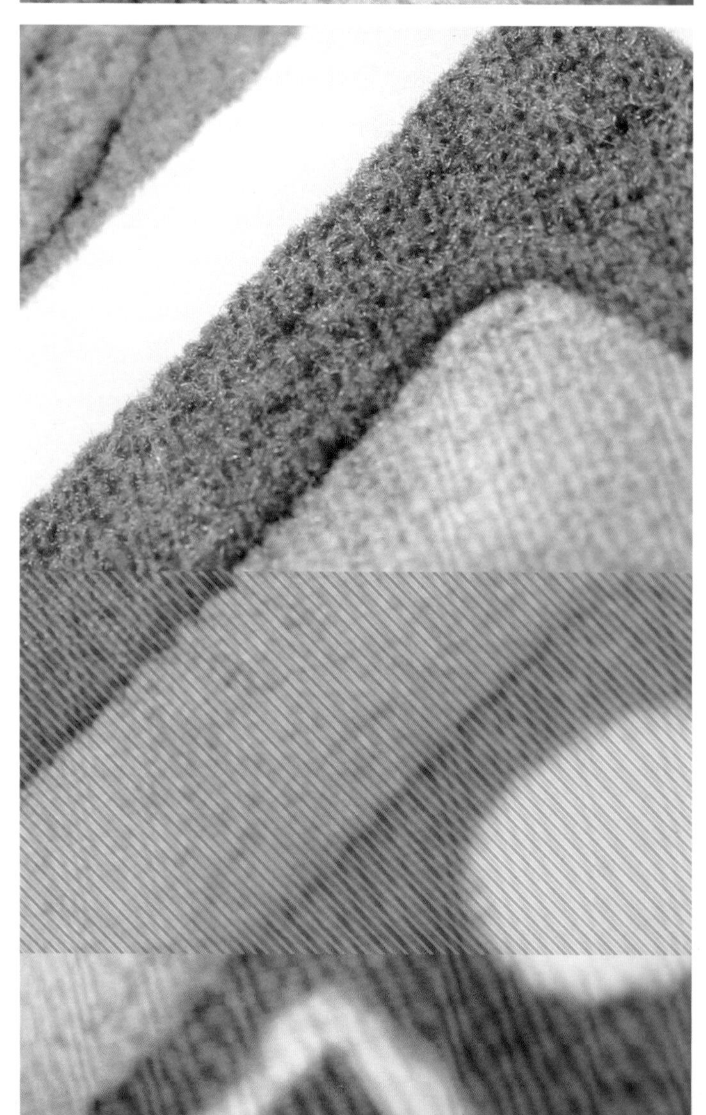

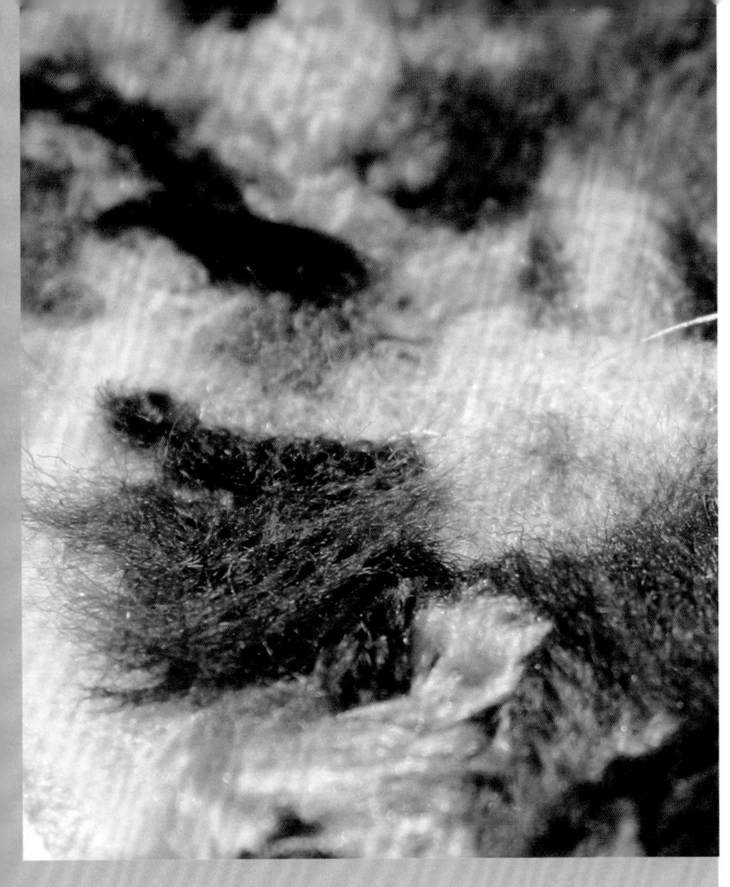

If using a backing fabric to work a dense area I suggest using a contrasting colour. In this instance white felt was used so that it was easy to see gaps in the piece and fill them in. This is why I find Caldo so useful. Tiny slivers can be pulled off and worked in, without spoiling the layout. Initially, follow the lie of the yarns and then fill in any gaps.

At this stage the reverse will show definite lines of work which can quite ugly, however, this is the quickest way I have found to set the pattern or 'movement' of colour.

When completely filled in with colour they become less defined and much more integrated into the whole.

This last picture shows the finished reverse side which now has the look of hand-made felt. To reach this stage the piece described above was again placed under the needles and worked in many directions including circles. It is very satisfying to work on a piece like this. As the yarns become more and more embedded into the carrier fabric you increasingly feel as though you are making your own felt.

CHAPTER: 6

Knitting Is Back

Knitting Is Back

Knitting is something which until recently I had only done under sufferance. Years ago I knitted many items, enjoying the technique and finishing all sorts of items. However in recent years I have found that it makes me very tense.

Yes, I know that most people find it relaxing, but it really does seem to have the opposite effect on me! Since the acquisition of my embellisher, though, I have found that I am turning more and more to the needles! I still find it makes me tense if I knit for any length of time, but I have evolved a technique that I can use in conjunction with the embellisher and only knit for a short time. The piece overleaf was made using this technique. Any yarn can be used, the one that I chose is a lightweight manmade yarn with knobbles and glittery bits.

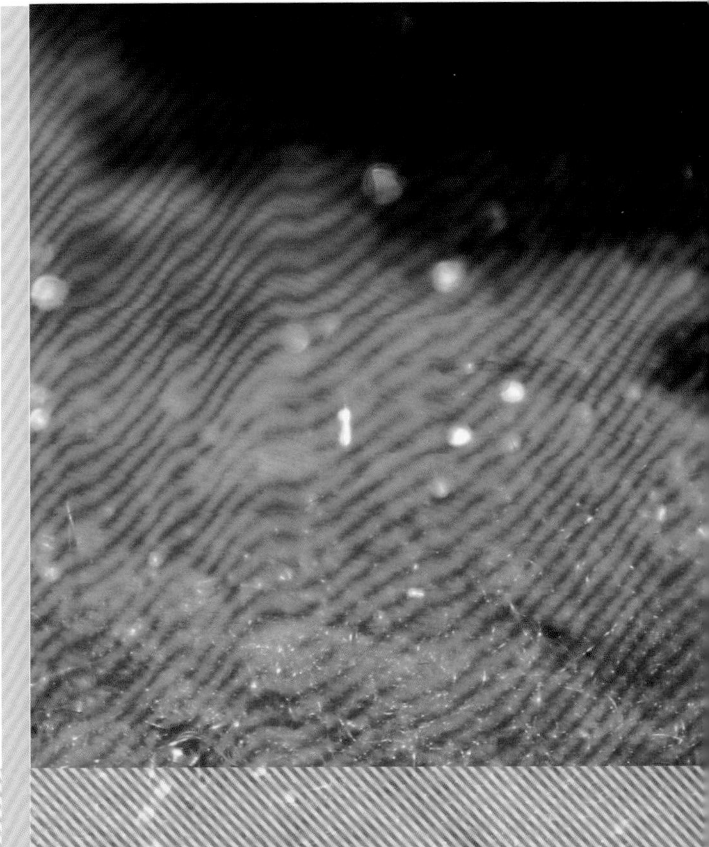

Using knitting needles that are two sizes larger than those recommended for the yarn I cast on twenty-five or so stitches (the number is immaterial). Then I cast off!! I call this a 'flag', and it's as simple as that. I leave a couple of inches before starting again – cast on more stitches, maybe only eleven this time, and cast off.

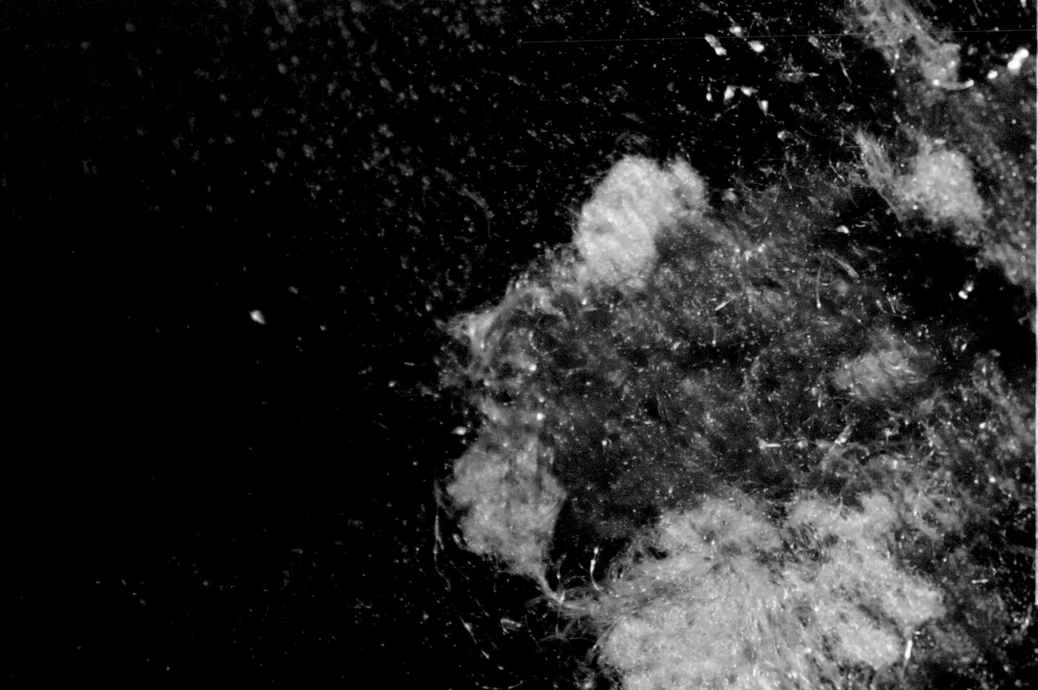

So there is no time to get tense! I can put it down at any time and if the needles are short I can knit anywhere. I have even been known to take them with me to use in the car when being driven on a long journey. It doesn't take long to build up a collection of half-knitted balls of yarn. When I need one I just cut the flag away and there is still another ready for next time.

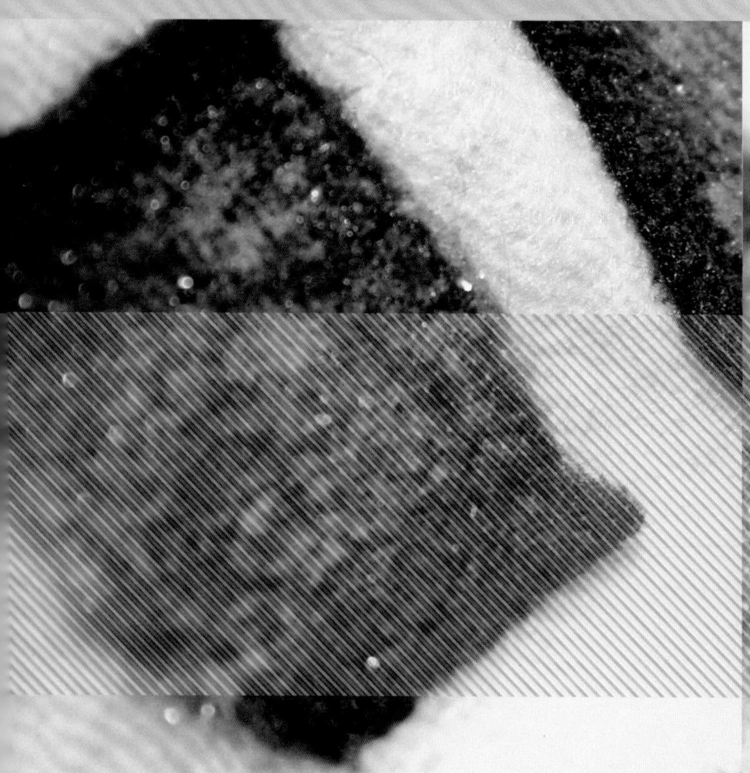

A pink 'flag' was meshed onto royal blue acrylic felt; this was then cut into random squares. The reverse of the strip was as interesting as the front, so three of each side were combined with squares of the original blue felt and arranged. Placed on Yellow felt and meshed together they seemed to 'sing'.

However, the reverse of the design was totally unexpected.

Finger knitting is another way of preparing yarn for embellishing. There are several techniques for this, but the one that seems the most popular is as follows.

Ignore your thumb. It is useful for holding any stray yarn in place, so don't 'occupy' it with a stitch!

1. Yarn is first wound around each finger.
2. Start with the little finger and make sure that the winding is fairly loose. It will be difficult to work the first 'row' if it is too tight.
3. Push these 'stitches' to the bottom of your fingers.

The next step:

4. Wrap the yarn right round the hand.
5. Try to keep this wrap above the 'stitches' previously formed, it will make it easier.

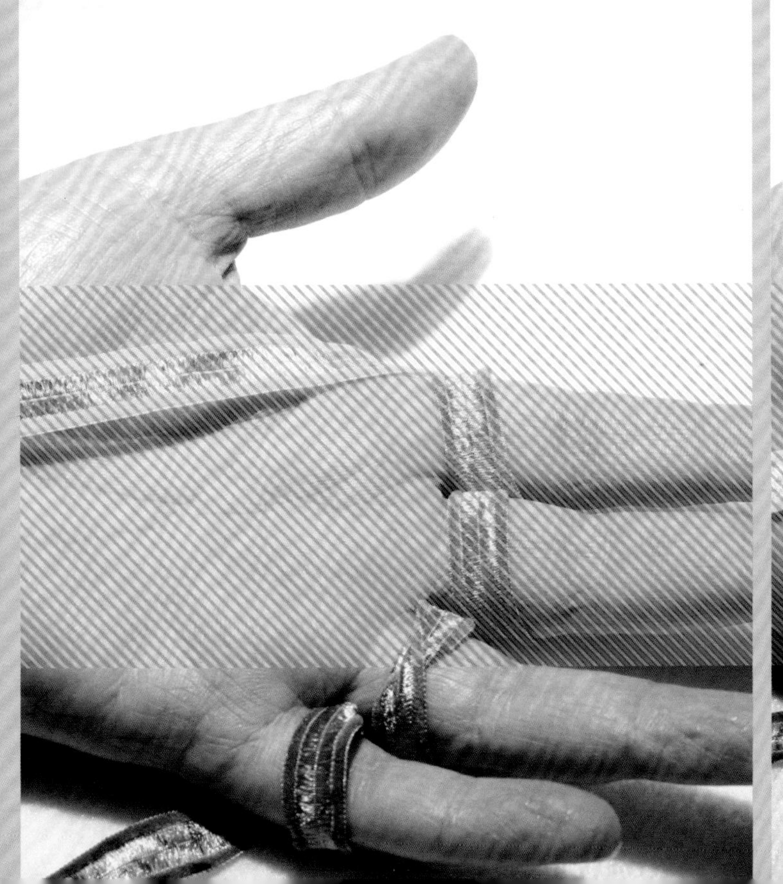

Starting with the little finger, and with palm facing:

6 Lift the loop up over the wrapped yarn and over the top of the finger to the back of the hand.

7 Continue in this fashion with each loop.

8 At the end of the 'row' there should still be a loop on each finger, and the knitting will start to grow behind your hand.

Another wrap of yarn and a further row of loop lifting continues the sequence.

Knitting Cast Off

9 When the cord is the length you desire it is time to cast off.

10 Lift the loop on the forefinger and move it onto the middle finger.

11 Take the original loop on the middle finger up and over as though knitting a stitch.

12 Transfer the remaining loop to the ring finger and knit a stitch in the same way.

13 Move this loop onto the little finger; knit it, only one loop now remains.

14 Slip the loose end of the yarn through the final loop and gently pull to secure.

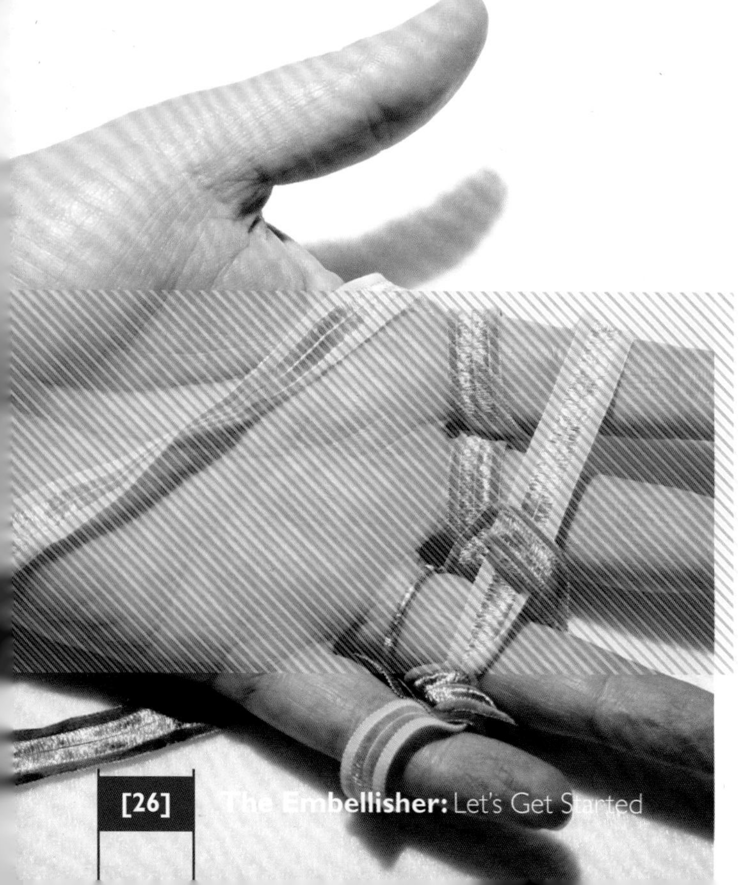

Eventually quite long lengths can be produced. These can either be applied to another surface or meshed in their own right. If you decide to try the latter a sandwich of SoluWeb will help to hold it in place whilst embellishing if you encounter any problems.

If you have a knitting machine you can knit pieces or lengths very quickly. These could then be decorated in various ways using the embellisher. Felting them, either by hand or in the washing machine before meshing would add yet another dimension to your work. The resulting fabric would make excellent clothing or soft furnishings.

CHAPTER: 7

Adding Your Own Colour

Adding Your Own Colour

In the chapter 'Working With Wool' I describe the technique of laying down yarns and meshing until the reverse looks like hand-made felt. A fun way to use the same technique is with plain white quilting wool - the end result will surprise you. Quilting wool is readily available from a number of outlets, especially quilting suppliers and from addresses listed at the end of the book.

First decide on your base fabric. When using this technique with an undyed yarn, dark fabric is a useful contrast. As you cover it with the quilting wool it will disappear leaving only the undyed yarn visible, until then it remains conspicuous and any that is still showing asks to be covered.

1. Lay down as much yarn as you need to cover the piece. If preferred you can cut smaller lengths and scatter them randomly.
2. Work into it lightly as you place the lengths just to hold them in place.
3. Once you have covered the whole area begin to work into it very well.
4. Turn the work over from time to time. If there is still a lot of dark fabric showing turn it back over and mesh it again.

When you are happy with the result try the following little experiment.

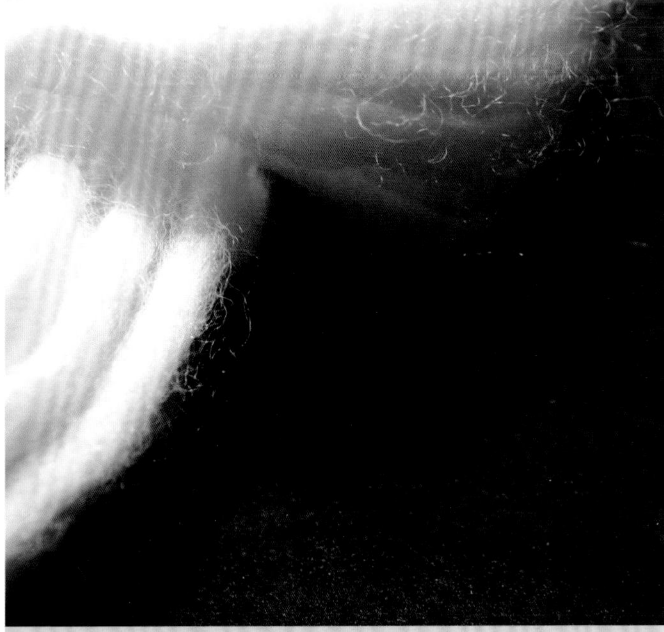

Experiment:

You will need:

- Microwave*
- Measuring jug*
- A microwaveable container with lid*
- A bowl or dish for soaking the fabric*
- Plastic spoon*
- 1 or 2 Syringes
- Oven gloves*
- Tongs for removing the dyed item from the hot dish*
- Water
- Distilled Malt Vinegar
- Rubber gloves (see note below)
- Food colourings of your choice (the pastes work just as well as the liquids but I have found it best to mix it with a small amount of vinegar water first).

*It is important to use a dedicated microwave and utensils if you wish to experiment with dyeing. This technique uses only materials that are found in the kitchen (*but do not use utensils etc that are subsequently to be used for food*). Develop good practice, even if only dabbling. Always take care, work in a well-ventilated area. Remember colours will stain, so wear rubber gloves when applying the dyes and handling unfixed items.

The instructions that follow are ideal for a small piece of fabric and particularly suited to wool (they won't work on cotton). Please read through them carefully before starting to dye.

Make sure that you have everything to hand before you actually start.

1. Carefully measure 100ml (½ cup) distilled malt vinegar into the jug.
2. Add 400ml (1½ cups) water. (The total quantity is now 500ml/2 cups.)
3. Place the bowl for soaking onto a firm surface.
4. Put the meshed fabric, into this.
5. Pour the vinegar/water mix over and leave it to soak.
6. Turn it over a few times.
7. Work the wetting solution into any dry areas using the back of the spoon.

This may take longer than you think! Don't try to rush, it is worth the wait.

When you are happy that the fabric is well soaked, transfer it carefully to the microwaveable container. DO NOT WRING IT OUT! It should be wet.

Now comes the fun part!

8. Using a syringe add drops of food colouring
9. Choose another colour and apply in the same way using a clean syringe. The colours will mix and are very intense
10. Work the colours in with the back of the plastic spoon remembering to rinse it between colours if necessary.

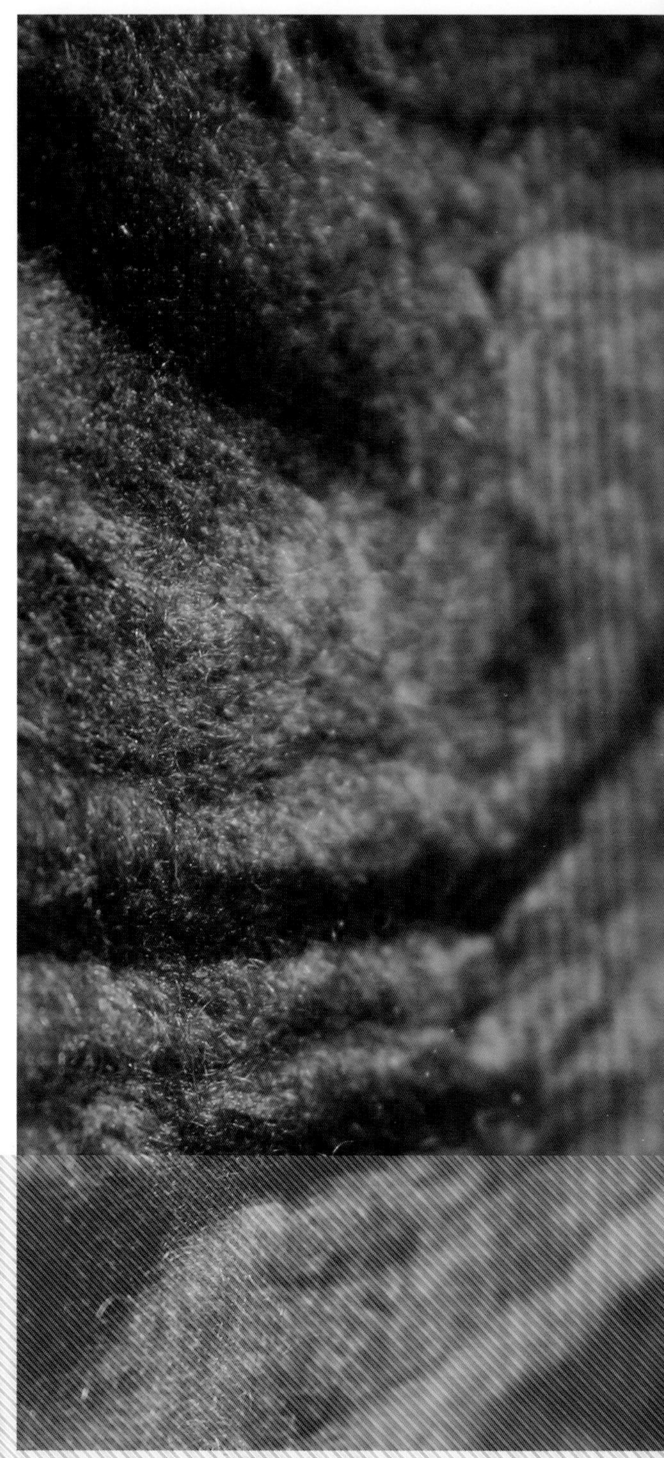

Now cover it with the lid and place in the microwave.

The container WILL get hot, so *use oven gloves at each stage*

11 'Cook' for one minute on High (650deg)*.

12 Leaving the lid on and using gloves, rotate the container a quarter turn.

13 Repeat on the same temperature for another minute.

14 Finally, quarter turn again and heat for a further minute.

15 Remove from the oven.

16 Still using oven gloves, carefully remove the lid. The process is a little smelly, mainly due to the vinegar, but the smell will soon rinse out of your sample.

*CAUTION

If 'cooked' for too long, or at too high a temperature wool WILL burn. (Burning wool smells even worse than the vinegar mix!)

Your plain white wool has been transformed. Using tongs carefully transfer it to a bowl of cold water and rinse well until the water runs clear. Squeeze out the excess water and leave to dry.

Once again, don't forget to look at the back! Sometimes it looks just like velvet. Contrasting black felt seems to be the key here. It creates shadows which give the piece a 3-dimensional quality.

CHAPTER: 8

Fabulous Fibres

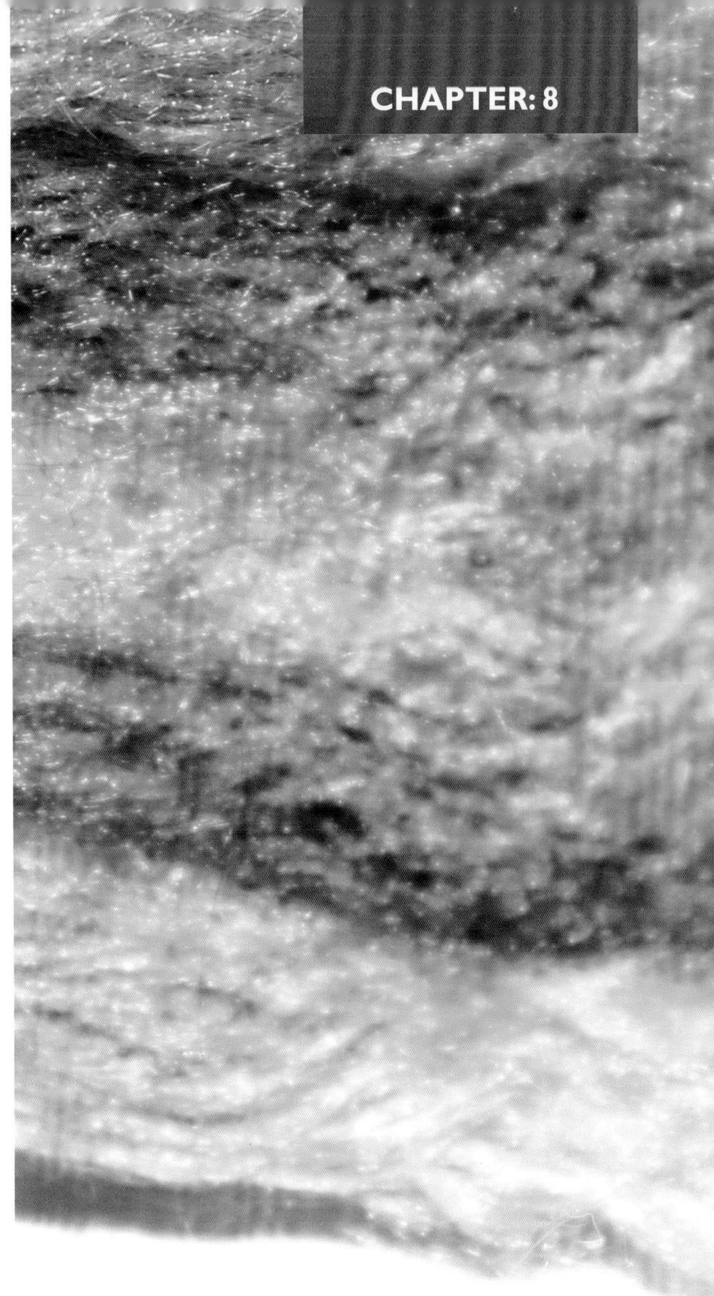

Fabulous Fibres

Wool is easy to felt. It is used in this form all over the world, and is often felted without mechanical means. Silk and viscose fibres, however, are more difficult to felt in this way, although they can be formed into a type of 'paper' by using the appropriate medium.

Angelina Fibres can be ironed to make similar sheets of 'paper', but using them under the needles of the embellisher has a completely different effect. Other fibres can be used too. Try soy, bamboo or hemp and anything else that springs to mind.

It is possible to mesh fibres on their own but beware of the needles! Fingers CAN get caught, in spite of the guard, if held too close to the needles. This is very tempting as fibres are quite bouncy and 'flyaway'.

A useful technique that I have found is to sandwich them between 2 layers of SoluWeb. This water-soluble fabric is gossamer fine. It is intended for use with knitted fabrics, its construction giving it a certain amount of flexibility. It is light enough to not interfere with the process of meshing, and if there is any remaining, it will disappear with a quick spray of water. Using SoluWeb also means that the lightest possible spread of fibres can be used.

Other water-soluble fabrics are suitable too, however these will usually need to be submerged in water, maybe more than once, to completely dissolve.

Fibres are equally interesting if placed on a background fabric before meshing. Try mixing a variety of fibres for extra texture, wool and viscose or silk will give an interesting matte and shiny effect and' for a little bit of glitz, Angelina could be added, There is no need to iron the Angelina first, just incorporate a few filaments with other fibres. The effect can be very subtle. A flamboyant effect is achieved by adding more filaments.

Try using a variety of backing fabrics.

New nappy liners, washed baby wipes or garden fleece can form lightweight materials.

Butter muslin or scrim will create very drapeable effects. Consider also loosely woven viscose or silk.

For a firmer surface use felt.

A heavier water-dispersible fabric such as AquaFilm, Romeo or SoluFleece could also be used, especially if the finished item is to be moulded over a bowl or other shape. The soluble fabric will completely disappear if soaked in water once meshing is finished, but only partly dissolving some of these dispersible fabrics enables the item to be moulded.

Another interesting effect can be obtained by meshing fibres into Mulberry Bark. Small pieces could be applied to another background, or incorporated into a freely stitched hanging etc.

Chiffon scarves too are an ideal backing.

Fibres meshed lightly or densely will create many effects.

Experiment until you are satisfied.

CHAPTER: 9

Nuvo Felt

Nuvo Felt

I was not expecting to discover NUVO FELT!

When playing around with a variety of yarns etc, I found large quantity of hand-dyed viscose fibres. These are soft and lustrous, and are available in a beautiful range of colours. I was trying to achieve, but how?

I arranged the fibres on a base fabric - they looked 'OK' but, in truth, as though they had just been 'plonked' down, not really integrated with the backing and far too heavy. I tried using the fibres under the needles with no base fabric, the fibres felted together easily, but the result was disappointing mainly because the soft fibres are difficult to control as they are pushed under the needles, and the resulting fabric much thicker than I wanted.

Now realising that 'control' was the key I returned to pre-made felt base and tried trapping the fibres under a dyed nylon chiffon scarf. This worked fairly well, but the colour of the felt changed the colour of the fibres and the resulting fabric was even thicker than I wanted.

A sudden brainwave reminded me of some white chiffon scarves I had hidden away. I tried the process again, and to my delight discovered that the colour of the viscose fibres was hardly altered at all. The scarf became invisible. My brain went into overdrive... ..."what if ....!" I grabbed another white chiffon scarf and cut it in half. I carefully arranged the fibres then sandwiched them with the rest of the scarf.

EUREKA!

That was the beginning, but there is more too it than that, so here began the exciting adventure that became NUVO FELT.

The first few stages are the most delicate. Once you have mastered them the process becomes quick and easy. This is the way that I work when making small pieces. Try this method then develop your own way of working

The embellisher is a light machine and therefore easy to move. I find it easier to perform the following first steps in front of the machine. Move the embellisher back so that there is enough space to place one piece of chiffon scarf flat on the table. The reason for this will become obvious shortly.

Basic Fabric

All you need is a supply of chiffon scarves (at least five layers) and some Viscose fibres in a couple of colours.

The fabric is made in seven stages.

STAGE ONE

Work in front of the machine, as previously described,

1. Place a single layer of chiffon scarf flat on the table.
2. Gently separate a small amount of fibres. Start in the middle top of the chiffon.
3. Lie the fibres on top, covering an area no more than 13cm square (approx 6 ins square). DON'T be any more ambitious that this at first! The fibres do not have to lie in one direction, nor do they have to overlap, but it doesn't matter if they do!!
4. Carefully place the second layer of chiffon over the fibres. You have now created a sandwich with filling in only a small area.

STAGE TWO

Your piece of 'raw' fabric is now at its most vulnerable.

5. Check that the embellisher is plugged in and ready for use, but *don't move it yet*! Check also that the needles are in the raised position.
6. Take hold of the sandwich carefully keeping it as taut and flat as possible. Hold it using the areas to the right and left of the fibres.
7. Gently lift, slide and guide the sandwich up onto the machine. Pass the area with the fibres under the needles ready to mesh.
8. Turn the wheel by hand so that the needles are in the fibres, then carefully lift the Embellisher forward into a comfortable working position, taking care that none of the chiffon is under the machine.

STAGE THREE

9 Gently stretch the sandwich, moving it in a variety of directions under the needles while the machine runs at a steady medium speed.

10 Work from back to front, side to side and in circles, concentrating on a small area at a time and then moving on to another.

11 Hold the sandwich firmly as you guide the sandwich around under the needles, meshing the fibres together. If you aren't careful you will find that the needles seem to 'eat' the chiffon and your resulting piece will be the size of a peanut!

Stop before you get to the edge of the fibres as you are now going to add more viscose. Don't worry if you forget while doing your practice piece.

STAGE FOUR

You will notice that the area you have meshed has become very stable. It can now be moved away from the machine and placed on any flat surface.

12 Lift the top layer of chiffon and add some more fibres. Try to keep the density and area about the same as before.

13 Replace the top chiffon layer and return it to the embellisher. Manipulate this section in the same way as before. The two areas should become one.

14 Repeat these last steps until you have filled the chiffon sandwich.

STAGE FIVE

Using fibres of another colour make a second piece of fabric in exactly the same way as above.

STAGE SIX

Now we get to the really exciting bit.

15 Take the pieces of fabric you have just made and cut them into random strips using scissors.

16 Don't use ruler and cutting wheel, if the edges curve slightly that is just fine!

17 Next cut your strips into random squares and rectangles.

STAGE SEVEN

We are now going to mesh our pieces onto the final layer of chiffon.

Starting in the middle of the scarf place a cut piece of your meshed fabric on top.

Move this under the needles and mesh thoroughly. You will need to hold the surrounding fabric very firmly, and work in various directions.

Place another cut piece onto the base layer close to the first and mesh as before. Work well into the adjoining edges.

Continue adding cut pieces and meshing well until you have used them all.

You have now completed your first piece of Nuvo Felt.

The finished fabric is similar in some ways to Nuno Felt, however the latter is made by a specific hand process and therefore a fabric in its own right. This is a new process created from man made fibres (including viscose) therefore I named it Nuvo Felt.

Nuvo felt is extremely flexible and could be used for a variety of purposes including clothing. It makes lovely scarves, bags and book covers which can be further embellished by hand or machine stitching and beads. It is easy to make larger pieces by adding other chiffon scarves and covering the joins with more meshed squares.

As you work the fabric you will find that it can also be manipulated into hills and valleys as described earlier. This is an alternative effect you may like to explore.

CHAPTER: 10

What Now?

What Now?

If you have worked your way through all the ideas in the book you will have acquired quite a large collection of samples. Uses for some will be obvious. Bags of all shapes and sizes need a firm fabric and we have seen that we can make a very firm fabric using the Embellisher.

Meshing alone, however, may not be enough for all uses of your experiments. Some may need further stitching, either to create a stronger surface, or just for further decoration. Beads, tokens and other additions can also be added for enrichment.

Lighter, flowing fabrics can be used for garments, scarves and shawls. Strengthening with adhesive backing and a firm fabric will make these also suitable for bags or book covers. These too could be further embellished as already mentioned. Consider too the addition of tassels, cords etc in sympathetic colours. You may also want to think about cutting some of your samples into a variety of shapes to reapply to other pieces of work.

For example a flower shape cut from a meshed fabric could be applied to a bag front and re-meshed, or just attached with a button or collection of beads.

A larger piece of fabric could be cut into strips or squares then re-assembled to take advantage of the texture on both sides. When remeshed it also could be used for a variety of purposes.

The ideas are endless, so hopefully these suggestions will not only inspire you to 'Get Started' but also to 'Keep Going'!

COURSES and WORKSHOPS

For details of courses etc please contact the author
or Missenden Abbey, Great Missenden, Buckinghamshire,
Telephone: 0845 045 40 40

SUPPLIERS

UK

Embellisher Project Packs, Chiffon scarves, SoluWeb, water-soluble and heat-dispersible fabrics, suitable knitting yarns, Angelina Fibres, Viscose Fibres, quilting wool

Winifred Cottage
17 Elms Road, Fleet, Hampshire, GU51 3EG
Telephone 00 44 (0) 1252 617667
www.winifredcottage.co.uk

For information on Lana Grossa Yarns:

Lana Grossa Yarns
Scottoiler, 2 Riverside, Milngavie, Glasgow, G62 6PL
Telephone 0141 955 1100
Email: sales@scottoiler.com
www.lanagrossa.co.uk

Supply of BabyLock Embellisher and various sewing machines etc.

Franklins Group Ltd
13-15 St Botolphs Street, Colchester, Essex, CO2 7DU
Telephone 01206 563955
Email: info@franklinsgroup.com
www.franklinsgroup.com

Further information on the BabyLock Embellisher:
www.babylock.co.uk

USA

Further information on the BabyLock Embellisher:
www.babylock.com

Chiffon Scarves, Angelina Fibres
Quilting Arts Magazine LLC, PO Box 685, Stow, MA 01775

AUSTRALIA

Further information on the BabyLock Embellisher
www.babylock.com.au

Chiffon Scarves, Angelina Fibres
The Thread Studio, 6 Smith Street, Perth 6000, Australia